Tips for parents and caregivers

Speak these words with enthusiasm!

Speaking affirmations is one of the most important things we can do for ourselves. Affirmations help to instill confidence, self-love and power in your child's life. Starting their day with declaring positive things about themselves is a great way to have a productive day. Repeating positive phrases shapes who we want to be and helps to create a positive world around us.

Aa

I am Amazing!

Bb

Beauty is all around me.

Cc

I can Create anything!

Dd

I am a Dreamer!

Ee

I **E**ncourage others.

Ff

I have a **F**antastic life!

Gg

I am Grateful for all I have!

Hh

I am **H**elpful.

Ii

I use my Imagination to create my reality.

Jj

My life is an incredible Journey.

Kk

I am Kind to others.

Ll

I Love myself!

Mm

All that I set my Mind to I will accomplish!

Nn

New ideas come to me daily!

Oo

I am **O**bservant.

Pp

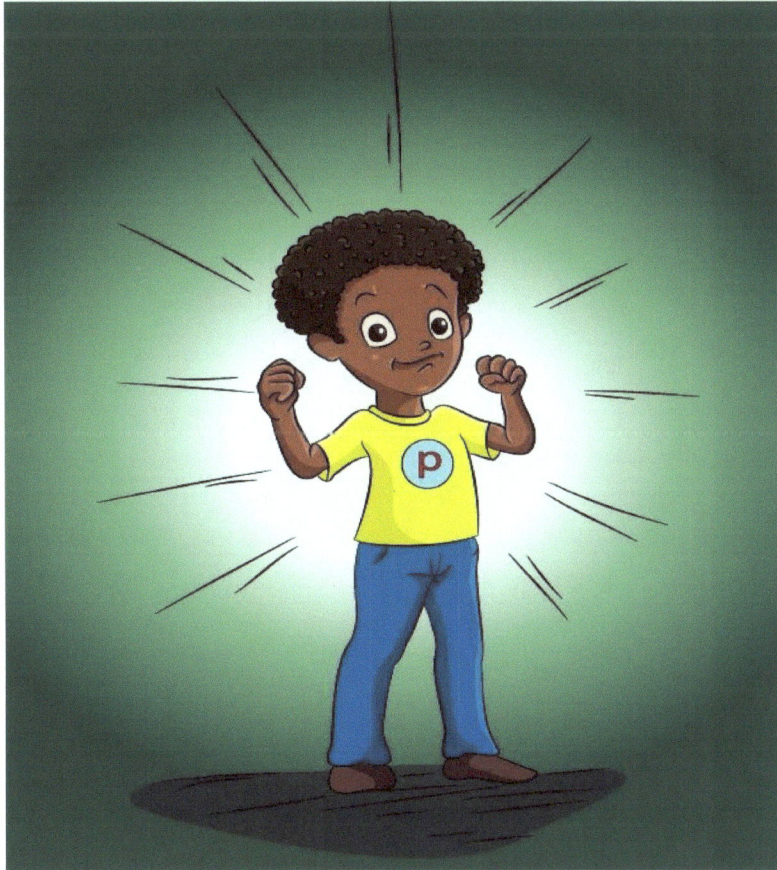

I am Powerful!

Qq

Quiet time is good for me.

Rr

I love to Read!

Ss

I have Sunshine in my heart!

Tt

I have many **T**alents.

Uu

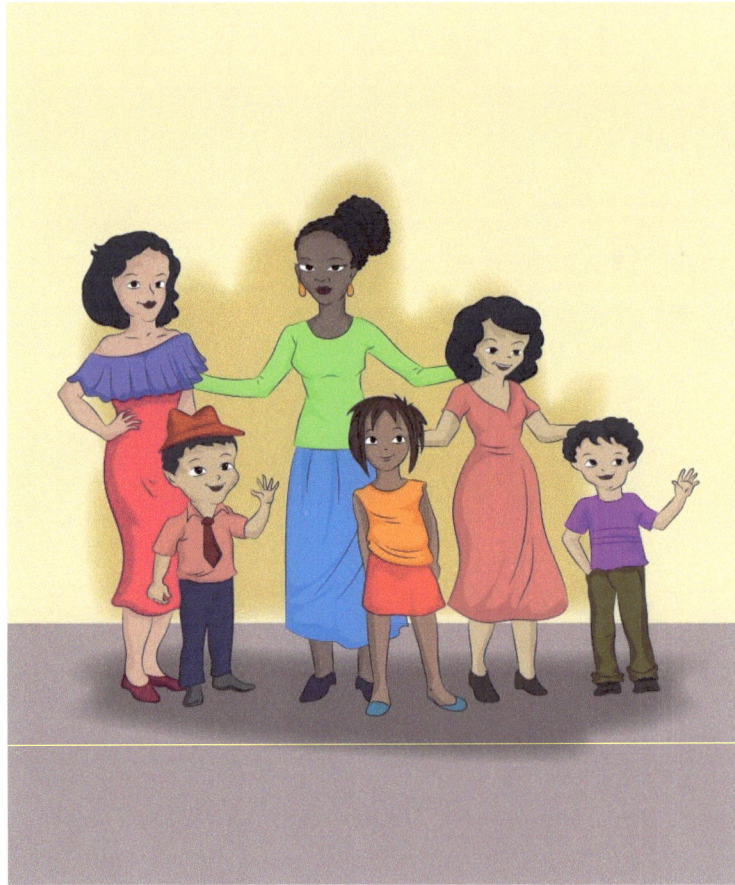

I am Unique!

Vv

I am **V**ictorious!

Ww

I make **W**ise decisions.

Xx

EXercise is great for my body.

Yy

I love You!

Zz

I am full of **Z**est!

A I am **A**mazing!
Amazing (ə meI zihng) - adjective
causing great surprise or wonder.
The stars look amazing!

B **B**eauty is all around me.
Beauty (byu-ti) – noun
The quality of being pleasant to the senses or
beautiful; loveliness.
The beauty of the music made us happy.

C I can **C**reate anything!
Create (kri-eIt) – verb
to bring into being.
The chef created new food.

D I am a **D**reamer!
Dreamer (drim-er) – noun
a person with a strong hope or goal.
Her dream is to become a doctor. She is a
dreamer.

E I **E**ncourage others.
Encourage (ihn-kuhr-ihj) – verb
to give help, support, or approval to.
Mom encouraged her to become famous.

F I have a **F**antastic life!
Fantastic (faen taes tihk) – adjective
excellent and incredible.
You are a fantastic singer!

G I am **G**rateful for all I have!
Grateful (greIt fəl) – adjective
feeling thankful or showing thanks for kindness.
I am grateful for your help.

H I am **H**elpful.
Helpful (help fəl) – adjective
giving help or aid.
You are very helpful around the house.

I I use my **I**magination to create my reality.
Imagination (ə mae jih neI shən) – noun
the power to create thoughts, pictures, or
images of something or someone in your mind.
She uses her imagination to write stories.

J My life is an incredible **J**ourney.
Journey (juhr ni) – noun
a long trip from one place to another.
The ship makes the journey across the sea.

K I am **K**ind to others.
Kind (kaInd) – adjective
helpful; friendly; good.
You were kind to that old lady.

L I **L**ove myself!
Love (luhv) – noun, verbs
strong feelings of affection or really liking a
person or thing.
I love my teddy bear!

M All that I set my **M**ind to I will accomplish!
Mind (maInd) – noun, verb
the part of you that thinks, understands,
remembers, directs, and feels.
Your mind is full of imagination!

N New ideas come to me daily!
New (nu) – adjective
not known before or something not used.
I got a new book today!

O I am Observant.
Observant (əb zuhr vənt) – adjective
to watch carefully; alert; attentive.
I was observant and could see she was upset.

P I am Powerful!
Powerful (paU ər fəl) – adjective
having or able to use power or force.
The race car is very powerful!

Q Quiet time is good for me.
Quiet (kwaI iht) – adjective
making no sound or noise.
The baby is very quiet when she sleeps.

R I love to Read!
Read (rid) – verb
to speak aloud something written or to
understand the meaning of words.
I love to read new books.

S I have Sunshine in my heart!
Sunshine (suhn shaIn) – noun
the bright light of the sun.
I love the feeling of sunshine on my face at the
beach.

T I have many Talents.
Talent (tae lənt) – noun
a natural skill or ability.
He has a talent for dancing and playing music.

U I am Unique!
Unique (yu nik) – adjective
being the only one of its kind and different from
everything else.
Everyone's fingerprints are unique.

V I am Victorious!
Victorious (vihk tor i əs) – adjective
having won; to be a winner
I won the spelling bee contest and was
victorious!

W I make Wise decisions.
Wise (waIz) – adjective
having understanding and good judgement
about what is true.
The old man is very wise.

X EXercise is great for my body.
Exercise (ek sər saIz) – noun, verb
activity done to keep the body and mind strong.
Swimming is good exercise and reading is great
exercise for the mind.

Y I love You!
You (yu) – pronoun
the person or persons being spoken or written
to.
You are reading this and you are special.

Z I am full of Zest!
Zest (zest) – noun
a sense of great pleasure or enjoyment.
My grandmother's zest for living makes her
seem much younger.

Source: https://kids.wordsmyth.net/we

For Alphie: Mommy loves you.

This book is dedicated to Brenda Carson and Margaret Weekes. Your love, lives and legacies live through us.

Thank you Aranahaj Iqbal (aranahajart.com) and Joe Pallante (joesenglishcafe.com) for your help in bringing this book to life.

A special thank you to my wonderful husband Nick. This book wouldn't be possible without your infinite patience and support.

About the Illustrator

Aranahaj Iqbal has been illustrating for over six years and has many published books. She enjoys illustrating children's books. She also provides illustrations for book series, single books, and long-term projects. You can visit her on Facebook @aranahajart, Instagram @aranahajiqbal and Twitter @AranahajI and website www.aranahajart.com to see her portfolios.

About the author

Sharlisa is an adventurer, creator and lover of life. She loves traveling, worldschooling her daughter and being an amazing wife. Her passion is inspiring others to live their best lives. She's written books on moving abroad and other works on being great to yourself. Her motto is "Your Life, Your Terms". Stay tuned for upcoming books in this series.

www.ingramcontent.com/pod-product-compliance
Lightning Source LLC
LaVergne TN
LVHW072059070426

835508LV00002B/178

9 781733 393508